A to Zillion

Managing Her Dementia and Remembering Our Lives Before

Written By
Susan Byrne-Wickey

Page Intentionally Left Blank.

Copyrights

Dedication

I dedicate this piece of writing to everyone mentioned in these pages. Your kind presence, whether through regular or occasional visits, thoughtful gestures, and dedicated efforts, has made a significant difference in this fragile yet whimsical pursuit of a quality life for Sheila.

About the Author

I drew my inspiration for A to a Zillion not from theory, but from the heartfelt experience of caring for Sheila, a beloved yet headstrong family member living with dementia and Alzheimer's. What began as a personal struggle with frustration, fear, and absurdity evolved into a memoir centered on survival, dark humor, and unexpected tenderness.

Over time, my writing shifted from simple reflection to intentional expression. It started as a collection of personal journal entries—a way to navigate the reality of caregiving—and gradually transformed into a book. Woven throughout are glimpses of life before the caregiving years—reminders of how love, family, and memories gave us the strength and capacity for what came after.

Thus, this writing serves as more than just a record of caregiving; it also reflects identity, endurance, and the moments that revealed who we truly were when life demanded everything. Using each letter of the alphabet as a chapter heading provided a scaffold for aligning the themes and insights within my writing. It helped me organize the unspoken moments and, in doing so, discover my voice amid the flow. Along the journey, I found that even during tough times, you're not alone—there is solidarity in the struggle, and sometimes, even calm.

Table Of Contents

Preface

If I knew then what I know now... is the heartbeat of this memoir. For those of you just starting out, still trying to make sense of the diagnosis, chaos, and exhaustion that come with managing someone with dementia, or more specifically, Alzheimer's, this memoir provides a little foreshadowing—not to scare you or make it heavier, but to help you feel a bit more prepared than I was.

And for those nearing the end, or deep in the thick of it— I hope you read these pages and think, I'm not alone. Because you're not. There are zillions more things to do. There always will be. But you don't have to do them alone.

Introduction

Before dementia changed her, there was only Sheila — my husband's older sister, a dynamic and dramatic character with many talents. She had been woven into our story long before caregiving entered the picture: joining us on our honeymoon with Mum, sharing birthdays, holidays, and other moments big and small. My husband, Tony, our daughters, Christie and Monyca, and our son, Will, all carried our snapshots of Sheila: vibrant, spirited, commanding, and entirely herself. We begin her story and ours here.

Sheila

Sheila, twelve years Tony's senior, lived what could only be called an exotic life—full of fast cars, experimental drugs, and bold behavior. She would parade around the house in nearly see-through pants, just enough to reveal the pattern of her underwear.

She didn't hide who she was. She was very comfortable in her skin.

At her high school graduation, Sheila was awarded a scholarship to UCLA for her exceptional talent in art, but she turned it down to become a go-go dancer in Hollywood. That decision set the tone for her early life: bold, unpredictable, and untamed. The cover of this book features her self-portrait.

Tony and I

Tony recalled childhood memories of visiting Sheila in Los Angeles. He was just a little boy watching his older sister whirl around a big city—he understood what was happening. He read encyclopedias for fun. He was a quiet observer.

As a teen, Tony had a large paper route. It stretched from our neighborhood above Route 66 in Claremont down into the streets below. After he quit the route, my brother Tim and I took it over. Tim was younger than I, but he was a boy and confidently navigated the more questionable streets without hesitation. I appreciated his bravery.

My side of the paper route just so happened to include Tony's house.

Tony didn't know me yet. But in a roundabout way, that paper route became the first thread in the web that would eventually bring us together.

One day, while Tony was cleaning his aquarium, he saw me ride by, tossing a bound newspaper wrapped in a rubber band from house to house. "What?" he thought. A girl delivering papers?" That moment stuck with him. It was unexpected, unusual, and possibly historic.

That was the beginning of a relationship that would span almost 50 years, from teenage glances on paper routes to building a life, a family, and eventually a caregiving operation for Sheila on our land.

Our Honeymoon

Before Sheila got married, she and her mother—Tony⊠s mother as well—joined us on our honeymoon.

Yes, really. Our honeymoon.

After spending a few days alone in West Maui, just the two of us as newlyweds, we were ready for the next leg of our adventure: East Maui, Hāna. The real Hawaii.

And that was when they joined us.

A mother, a sister, and us, fresh from "I do."

Tony and I sat in the back of the pickup truck, got stoned, and became completely immersed in the rainforest and tropical jungle along the windy Hāna Highway that led us to Hāna.

It was dark when we arrived.

Sheila and Mum, "Mum," as I always called her, since she was from England and she wanted it that way, were furiously sweeping, jumping over large, live cockroaches on the floor, and crying loudly in the house. It wasn't really a house. It was a shack. A dirty one. The boys Sheila had known for years hadn't swept or lifted a finger before we arrived.

Tony and I were in the back of the pickup truck in the front yard, and that's where we planned to sleep our first night. A terrible idea, in retrospect. We got eaten alive by mosquitoes.

I think Mum took pity on us-or maybe she just couldn't stand seeing the welts all over our bodies—and decided to buy us a couple of nights at the Heavenly Hāna Inn. It was wonderful.

After the honeymoon, Mum returned home to California, while Sheila stayed in Hāna, met someone new, fell in love, got married, and settled in the caretaker's cottagewhere they managed the estate of Frank Herbert, the author of Dune.

But let's not get ahead of ourselves.

Cyndy

Instead of accompanying Mum back to California after the honeymoon, Sheila decided to stay in Hāna—in that dilapidated, dirty shack she and Mum had cleaned up and made beautiful again. Sheila was a boss; she could get things done.

Bill and Jim had made no effort to clean the house before her arrival, so she put them to work the moment Mum left Maui. The house was nearly ninety years old, weathered and imperfect. It wasn't the kind of home she believed she deserved, but it had character—deep, remarkable character. She had lived there once before with her younger sister Cyndy, and she knew the spirit of the place by heart.

Sheila adored her little sister, fierce and protective like a mother bear with her cub. Years later, after they returned to the mainland to follow different paths, Cyndy was killed in a car accident—on a rainy Valentine's Eve, a tragedy that came unexpectedly. She was only twenty-six, while Tony and I were just twenty. Everyone was devastated.

Sheila rarely spoke about that night, but the loss rearranged her from the inside out. There was a tenderness in Sheila that never fully returned and a sharpness that sometimes cut without warning. It was grief, loneliness, and a love with nowhere to go. We could still feel her ache pulsing a decade later and a few more decades after that.

Bart

The house Sheila and Cyndy once lived in was an old plantation home, featuring a covered porch, spacious front and back yards, and fruit trees all around. Since her return, and after the boys cleaned up the place, Sheila sensed that something new and very special awaited her, and she was ready for it.

It was Jim who introduced her to Bart. Tall, blonde, and every bit the surfer from Santa Cruz, Bart was working construction with Jim in Hāna. Sheila arrived to meet him wearing a sexy, stylish sundress that showcased her rich tan and auburn hair. She knew exactly what she was doing. She had a bag of tricks that guys always fell for—especially the tall, blonde ones.

Sheila put on quite a show for Bart, and he fell head over heels for her. She was six years older than him and more than a foot shorter, but that didn't matter. During their initial attraction phase, Sheila wore large sun hats and cute bikinis that complemented her petite frame. She pretended to play tennis and made swimming in the ocean seem like part of her daily routine. They went on jungle picnics, sipped cold tropical cocktails, and lived in the soft-focus glow of new love.

Once Sheila sealed the deal with Bart, they got married, and she returned to painting. She continued to wear eye-catching outfits and bikinis, but the sparkle was only the beginning of the narrative.

Bart was a beer-drinking, blue-collar worker. Sheila was a tea-drinking painter and artist. Once the courting ended, so did the acting.

Even though the first phase of their relationship had ended, their life together remained rich and loving, dramatic, sultry, and filled with genuine connection and engaging conflict. They continued to maintain a vibrant sex life.

Bart became a contractor, building homes and a steady future. Sheila perfected her art, layering more creativity, color, and daring into her work as the years passed. They built their own house in Nahiku and invested their love in a captivating, beautiful life full of passion and commitment.

It was a brutal ending for Bart — colon cancer took him far too soon. But his memory lives on in Sheila's heart. Even now, even through the heavy fog of dementia, you can still see it — the way her spirit lights up when she hears his name, the way she catches her breath with her hand on her chest when she sees his picture.

Christie

Christie is Sheila's niece, our eldest daughterShe is eight years older than her sister, Monyca. Christie is vivacious, fun, and endlessly compassionate. She is a beautiful wife, a wonderful mother, a fabulous sister, and a deeply loving daughter.

Her connection with Sheila goes way back. And their history runs even deeper.

After the honeymoon ended, Tony and I returned home to Chico, California. On my birthday, we conceived Christie after a bonfire that turned into a fake barbecue grill when the fire department arrived. It was quite a spectacular beginning for our first daughter.

After Christie was born and ten months had passed, Sheila invited us to live in her caretakers' cottage on Frank Herbert's estate, which she and Bart managed. She accommodated us in their home on the living room floor for about two weeks—just enough time for us to catch our breath, feel the island beneath our feet, and imagine a life here.

We soon found a place of our own.

Christie was easygoing and delightful—true sunshine. She and Sheila got along famously. This marked the beginning of their relationship, one that would stretch, evolve, and remain strong for the next four decades.

Monyca

Warm, kind, and genuinely nice, Monyca was the type of person who made space for others—who spoke up for the things that mattered to her, always with a calm, considerate, and convincing tone.

Monyca was born at home in Kipahulu, East Maui, surrounded by jungle, waterfalls, and the sound of the sea. Sheila has known her since day one.

In fifth grade, Monyca chose to homeschool. She wanted to sew, learn to sing, and run her own business. Sheila volunteered as one of her teaching instructors and taught her how to use a sewing machine to create eye-catching clothing and swimsuits, and paint portraits with style.

Since then, Monyca has enjoyed a long and loving relationship with Sheila. Their bond has remained genuine, steady, and gentle for over thirty years.

Will

Will is our only son.

When I was nineteen, I gave birth to him and placed him for adoption. I believed I had to. I was Catholic and not married. I was steeped in dogma, shaped by it, and convinced that giving him up was the only right thing to do—a loving, faithful, responsible act I could offer.

I have carried that choice with me for decades.

And then, when he was thirty and expecting his first child, he reached out. No words are grand enough to capture what that moment meant to me, to Tony, to us. To be contacted by our first child after thirty years and invited back into his life, just as he and his wife, Franziska, were becoming parents themselves—it was beyond anything Tony or I ever imagined.

After their baby was born, Tony and I traveled to Colorado to meet Will, Franziska, and baby Benjamin. Some years later, Will and his family came to Maui to meet the rest of our family in Hāna at Monyca's wedding. This event marked Will's first meeting with Sheila. Although there were too many miles between them to foster the kind of relationship his biological sisters had with her, Will got to know Sheila better as time passed. When he learned she had Alzheimer's, he was there for us with an encouraging tone that felt like a warm hug.

Chapter A

Alzheimer's is a Brain Disorder

Alzheimer's disease is the most common cause of dementia, affecting millions worldwide. It is a progressive brain disorder that gradually destroys memory and thinking skills. The disease is characterized by the buildup of abnormal proteins in the brain, leading to nerve cell death and a decline in cognitive function. While early symptoms may include mild forgetfulness, the disease eventually impairs a person's ability to perform even the simplest tasks. Ongoing research continues to explore various avenues for effective treatments and, ultimately, a cure. National Institute on Aging. (2023). What Is Alzheimer's Disease? Retrieved from www.nia.nih.gov

Physical Confrontation

Physical confrontation often results from Alzheimer's in many patients due to feelings of being out of control, misinterpreting the behaviors of others, and feeling unheard or misunderstood.

While living on our property, Sheila confronted three people.

David

The first incident involved David, our yard maintenance guy—a Hawaiian gentleman in his early 60s who had maintained our property and Sheila's beautifully for years.

One day, David was weed-eating near her trailer, minding his own business, but Sheila didn't like it. She came running down the stairs and swung at him several times before clocking him in the arm.

Moments later, David appeared at our doorstep. His expression was serious.

"I'm going to call the police," he said.

It wasn't a threat; it was a line, and we knew he had every right to draw it.

We explained that Sheila's dementia had worsened since the time he maintained her property, and that these aggressive traits weren't personal—they were part of the disease.

I could tell that he was as sad as he was angry. He and his wife, Pua, used to roll up her driveway with all their equipment, and Sheila would run out of her house to greet them. Bart had already passed, and Sheila was living alone. In the years before she had Alzheimer's, she welcomed company.Sometimes, she would invite Pua inside to have tea and "talk story".

We told him we'd take care of it and that he should focus on another part of the yard. Thank goodness we managed to keep him—his work was excellent, and he was a man of quiet integrity—the kind you don't come across too often.

Shelley

Before my sister Shelley was diagnosed with throat cancer, she drank heavily. Wanting to help, she offered to be a companion to Sheila for a few afternoons.

Shelley thought the first visit went well. However, Sheila didn't share that sentiment. When Shelley returned to the trailer for a second time, Sheila made her disapproval clear. "Don't come in!" she shouted from the top of the stairs.

Shelley did not listen.

She thought she could charm her way through it and convince her that it would be fun. She always kept a few beers stashed in her bag—maybe for courage, maybe for comfort. It wasn't the first time Shelley had brought alcohol.And Sheila remembered the previous occasion all too well.

Sheila was furious, but this time she didn't just say no—she took action.

She stormed down the stairs, shouting for Shelley to leave, and attacked her. She scratched Shelley's arm severely, hit her, and shoved her back with surprising strength that no one expected from someone of Sheila's age, size, or condition.

Shelley was utterly astonished, heartbroken, and deeply afraid.

She had no idea Sheila was capable of that kind of rage, or that Alzheimer's could feel so violent, so personal, and so out of control. When Shelley came to my office door, she was shaking. I said, "Do you want me to take a picture of that scratch for the police?" She replied with giant blue eyeballs wide, "No!" Shelley feared retaliation would follow. I embraced her gently and brought her inside.

Honoré

The third time Sheila attacked someone occurred on our croquet course.

Sheila roamed the property daily, pacing and wandering restlessly. One day, she was making her way toward our house quickly when our primary caregiver, Honoré, intervened, attempting to redirect her path with calm words and soothing body language.

However, Sheila refused to accept it. Instead, she lunged at Honoré and attacked her by pulling her hair, knocking her sunglasses off her face, and breaking them.

They weren't just any sunglasses; they were Maui Jim's—expensive, a gift from me to Honoré. I had ordered them for myself, but couldn't wear them since I needed progressive lenses. Honoré looked like a movie star in them, and now they were shattered, just like the moment.

The Doctor Visit

Due to Sheila's increasingly aggressive—and sometimes outright vicious—behavior, my husband and I took her to the doctor. We needed a written diagnosis and thought it would be simple: describe what was happening and receive confirmation to determine the proper next move.

Instead, we were informed that a complete series of steps was required before any formal diagnosis could be made.

That day, while sitting in the exam room, I realized this would not be easy. It was going to be lengthy, and I had no idea what to expect.

Sheila, meanwhile, acted silly. She was flirtatious, constantly shifting moods, and sharing wildly inappropriate personal stories. She told the doctor, loudly and proudly, that she smoked pot with the construction workers at her house. Then, she launched into more ramblings, some funny and most just strange.

I observed with raised eyebrows.

The doctor didn't flinch. He listened with kindness and attentiveness. When he finally looked my way, he said, "She's trying to communicate the only way her brain allows."

It wasn't a diagnosis, but it marked the beginning.

Then he said something I hadn't expected. He confronted her with the truth, "You have Alzheimer's," he told her, gently but directly.

It was fascinating to watch her reaction. She didn't seem to care. Didn't protest. Didn't show fear.

She simply smiled vaguely and nodded, as if he had told her something trivial or unrelated.

She didn't seem to comprehend what he was saying.

And this was a woman who was once profoundly intelligent, well-read, articulate, and a talented artist. Now, the words just floated past her.

That was when I realized her days living alone in her home were numbered.

Chapter B

Behavior

How Her Behavior Affected Mine

Caring for someone with Alzheimer's involves managing behaviors that can test your patience and emotional stability. Sheila, in particular, exhibited many behaviors that caused me distress and influenced how I responded to her. I often found myself withdrawing or reacting with fear to her actions, especially when she appeared unexpectedly at our house and started stalking us.

The Olympic Champion

She was fast—like, freakishly fast. It felt like she could cover the distance from her place on the property to ours in two seconds flat—and she was in her late seventies. I started calling her the Olympic Champion. No training, no warm-up. Just sheer willpower and a burst of determination that could've taken down a linebacker.

The second I saw her making that beeline up the hill, I sprang into action: locked the doors, shut the drapes, and hid to make the house look uninhabited. Because if she made it to a window or door, she'd start moaning-eerily and repeatedly—

"Help! Help! Help!" like she was possessed. No amount of reasoning could stop it. She didn't seem to register that she was home, safe, with family.

And me? My heart would jackhammer in my chest. My hands would shake. I could feel every nerve in my body revolt. It felt like a nervous breakdown... except it happened in slow motion, daily, for nearly a year.

Chapter C
Coping, Claws, and Caregivers

Caregiving is emotionally taxing, and at times, the weight of it all can feel like a never-ending struggle. It's crucial to allow yourself to take a break and recharge, even if it's just by enjoying a hard seltzer.

White Claws

When Sheila was still living alone, we didn't call her condition Alzheimer's—not yet. We knew she was suffering from dementia, the damage caused by a lack of oxygen from the Christmas before. She had collapsed at our home on Christmas Eve and was rushed to the hospital by ambulance, where she stayed for five days. After she returned home, things were never quite the same.

Back then, my daughters, friends, and I showed up regularly at her house armed with love and snacks, like we were visiting a quirky aunt instead of walking into the slow burn of something irreversible. We brought a picnic basket full of nutritious food to keep things light. But we also had an ice chest packed with a rainbow of White Claws. That was for us.

Lime, black cherry, mango, raspberry—we tried them all. The hard seltzers became part of our ritual. After dealing with whatever mess or confusion the day had delivered—cat poop in the bathtub, microwave disasters, forgotten conversations—we'd sit down, open a can, and exhale a long sigh of relief.

It wasn't just a drink; it was a line in the sand—a way to claw back a little bit of us from the chaos of her.

My Caregiving Daughters

We all have our methods for managing stress, and sometimes, the little rituals make the hardest days feel bearable. Reflecting on how humor and simple indulgences helped us navigate caregiving shows that it's okay to lean into those moments for some relief.

Christie

After forty years of positive encounters with Sheila, Christie became one of her weekly volunteer caregivers.

Their long history didn't shield her from Sheila's moods. On some days, Sheila is warm and friendly, even playful. On others, she was fiercely obstinate—sharp-tongued, resistant, and mean.

Christie had no patience for meanness. She didn't deserve it. There's nothing in their shared past that would justify it. No unresolved tension. No old grudge. Just forty years of connection and care.

But this is what dementia does: it scrambles the map. The people who show up anyway—especially those who have been there all along—often take the hardest hits.

Before Sheila moved to our property, Christie often accompanied me to Sheila's house with her bright and beautiful child, Rylee. She and I would indulge in White Claws after a harrowing day of cleaning and listening to Sheila's demands to "Stop it!"

Once, after looking everywhere, she and Rylee, who was four years old, found Sheila's dead cat hidden in a stack of boxes under the kitchen table. This was one of the two cats Sheila had been tormenting with unique dinners like yogurt and cold fruit and making them pee and poo on magazine pages in the bathtub. These disturbing incidents did not kill the cat; Ginger was an old male cat who died of natural causes.

The dead cat hadn't been boxed up long, so there was no smell. After a thorough search, Christie finally found it packaged like Matryoshka dolls—a.k.a. Russian nesting dolls—only, thankfully, when she got to the last one, there was just one cat inside.

The four of them—Christie, Rylee, Sheila, and the boxed cat—proceeded to the yard. They dug a hole, gathered flowers, buried the cat, and held a little ceremony.

It was as bizarre as it was beautiful—a small act of kindness at the end of a very strange day.

Monyca

After more than three decades of fond memories with Sheila, Monyca also served as a caregiver. She approached the role with quiet strength. She didn't force things and wasn't easily rattled. In her better moments, Sheila appeared to respond to that ease.

While accompanying me on visits, Monyca brought her baby, Waiolu, with her—he was a big boy, bundled in a front pack, funny and full of light. Sheila would light up, too. We girls indulged in bubbly hard seltzers, and Monyca brought lunch or dessert.

Sheila delighted in the food and company but especially in the baby's sounds: the gurgles, the sudden giggles, and the clumsy flailing of little arms.

Even in the depths of decline, something in Sheila recalled what it meant to witness life unfolding. In those moments, something softened within her—something real and still within reach.

That's the thing about my daughters' visits. They often arrived, carrying the next generation in their arms, armored with the mettle to deal with Sheila's adversity.

Will

My son, Will, didn't provide care for Sheila; he didn't have to. He was there for me.

He'd say on the phone, "I know this must be so hard, Susie." Even if he only imagined what I was going through, he embraced me from afar with an empathetic and sincere tone that was steady, warm, and precisely what I needed.

That kind of love and understanding came from someone thousands of miles away who didn't know Sheila and who hadn't experienced our day-to-day lives but sensed my ongoing surrender to obligation.

It made all the difference.

My Caregiving Friends

Coping as a caregiver wasn't just about breathing exercises, prayer, or an occasional hard seltzer, though those had their place. Sometimes, the real coping came from veering way off topic — escaping into food, faraway ideas, jokes, science fiction worlds, or political debates about the president's executive orders. Anything that wasn't about dementia helped.

Linda

Linda was a caregiver for Sheila since the beginning of my journey—a volunteer, of course—because she had known Sheila as long as she had known me. She brought her intellect, humor, and delectable cuisine right along with her.

When we first met over forty years ago, Linda had been living in Maui with her partner, Frank, and their two young daughters, Lily and Iris. She always knew what she wanted and made no apologies for it. That is what I loved about her.

She would check out twenty books from the library at a time and lovingly read them to her kids. That kind of dedication left me in awe. She let them draw on the walls with crayons— something I didn't personally endorse, but the freedom of it still bedazzled me.

In those early days, cooking wasn't Linda's strongest suit. Fast forward 40 years to the present, and she became the kind of chef who could walk onto a set with Bobby Flay and hold her own. Talented, confident and improvisational—cooking from instinct, with flair and intent.

At the beginning of Sheila's dementia, Linda accompanied me to Sheila's house. I would bring the hard seltzers, and she would bring lunch. One time, she brought her own version of chile relleno—stuffed with tofu, of all things. I thought I was in heaven; it was so good. This was the same woman who once moved too fast in the kitchen, and now here she was, blowing me away with a dish fit to premiere on a cooking show.

Once Sheila moved onto our property, Linda couldn't commit to a weekly caregiving shift, but she visited as often as she could. Each time she came, she brought food that reminded us just how much love and care can be folded into a meal.

It wasn't just the White Claws at Sheila's house or Maui Hard Seltzers later that year at mine; it was the food and the fun — the comforting act of eating your fill, laughing while somersaulting on the couch, posing for photos in abandoned cars without tires, burned by arson, and graffitied with spray paint, and pretending for a few hours that real life wasn't happening.

Coping wasn't about fixing anything; it was about escaping the gravitational pull of dementia for a little while. It involved constructing tiny spaces in a collapsing world where food, laughter, creativity, and imagination could still thrive.

Gena

Gena, like Linda, had been my friend since the beginning of my adult life in Hāna, Maui. When we met, we were all young mothers in our early twenties.

Gena was a beautiful person with an extraordinary command of the English language—sharp, sensitive, and endlessly witty. We often engaged in intellectual discourse. She was progressive, imaginative, and articulate. Being around her made me feel mentally stimulated and amused.

We did some wild things together, including photoshoots in black see-through dresses and furs. We had big energy, bold ideas, and zero apologies. We even featured a fashion show at the Maui Arts and Cultural Center called "Wide Angle." Through it all, Gena remained a rare and brilliant friend—one who pushed boundaries and held space—the kind of person you never stop being grateful for.

Gena was the kind of friend who didn't need to be asked; she knew. When Sheila's memory started to fade, Gena accompanied me on visits to Sheila's house and then to the trailer on my property. After a couple of years had passed, Gena took a weekly shift on her own to visit Sheila in the Gallery.

Before her shift, Gena always stopped at our house to pick up a hot meal for Sheila and have a drink. Yes, you guessed it: a hard seltzer, but with her signature touch: a measured half shot of vodka and barely a splash of St. Germain. She sipped it with a sense of class—casual elegance, always—and made it last just long enough to accompany her walk down to visit Sheila.

When I was with Gena, coping was multifaceted. We spanned levels of consciousness. We debated science fiction concepts, explored the absurd, and had honest political conversations that drew me into other dimensions of thought— uncomfortable at times but constantly widening the airspace around me, allowing me to breathe beyond the tight circle of caregiving.

Gena brought ease, a touch of sparkle, and a sense that even amid all the chaos, style, friendship, and the eloquence of being present for Sheila mattered most.

Chapter D

Dignity and Dementia

Dementia leads to significant cognitive decline. Upholding Sheila's dignity, even when her behaviors challenged my patience and tolerance, was one of the most profound challenges of my life.

Recent research also shows that maintaining dignity is essential for improving the quality of life for dementia patients. A study published in The Lancet Neurology emphasizes that interventions focused on promoting dignity and autonomy can help reduce feelings of helplessness and depression that often accompany dementia. Caregivers play a crucial role in fostering a sense of dignity by validating the patient's experiences, even when their cognitive abilities may be compromised.

"Dementia does not rob someone of their dignity. It's our reaction to them that does." — Jean George.

Poem for Sheila

The most difficult thing about dementia
Is it that you can'tremember—that you can't remember
So, you feel lonely even after a visitor leaves,
because you can'tremember that anyone came.
And you think you haven't eaten,
even after receiving a warm meal,
because you can't remember that you ate it.
When you have dementia,
Your mind plays tricks on you,
making you suspicious of family and friends
and people who take care of you.
Your mind perseverates on the dark side.
You whine and cry and feel sorry for yourself
When nothing is wrong.
The family that cares for you is still familiar,
But they've become"those people" who live next door—
where, in your mind, you are not welcome.
But you are welcome!
And you are well taken care of.
You receive daily meals and visitors,
And you are loved.

Chapter E
Expectations

When you first become a caregiver for someone with dementia, it's essential to understand what to expect. Caregiving for a person with dementia is a complex, ever-changing journey that doesn't always fit the mold ofwhat you might imagine.

1. Expect that you will have or feel:

- Fear and anxiety
- Disappointment
- Sadness and grief
- Feelings of being trapped
- Overwhelming despair
- Longing to be free
- Wishing him or her gone
- Hopelessness
- Helplessness
- Increased desire to indulge

I wasn't caregiving. I was running a full-fledged rest home operation—with zero training, no handbook, and no pay.

I didn't anticipate the emotional toll—the fear, the despair, the longing to be free. But there it was.

I didn't expect the reported outbursts, the biting, the avoidance, or the long silences she presented to my helpers—but they came, too.

2. Expect to encounter:

- Inappropriate behavior
- Inconsiderate comments
- Incontinence and diapers
- Non-compliance
- Rudeness
- Unwillingness to cooperate
- Yelling and growling
- Unkind words
- Aggressiveness
- Biting
- Falling
- Refusing to shower
- Silent treatment
- Avoidance

I went into caregiving with a set of idealistic expectations, thinking I could handle it all and that things might improve with the proper care. But over time, I came to realize that caregiving for someone with Alzheimer's requires constant flexibility, self-compassion, and the recognition that barely anything is within your control. The disease is unpredictable, and as much as you may wish for things to improve, the reality is that you'll need to adjust your expectations regularly.

One of the most challenging lessons was recognizing that Tony and I couldn't handle everything alone and that asking for help wasn't a sign of weakness—it was a necessity. I had to be kinder to myself and acknowledge that caregiving was a shared responsibility. Reflecting on these expectations has been crucial for me in understanding how to better cope with the demands of caregiving. Ultimately, it helped me come to terms with the fact that the best I could do was to be present, show love, and give Sheila the dignity she deserved.

3. Expect to:

- Pay out of pocket
- Shop and order food and supplies
- Haul packages, unload, and store goods
- Manage bank accounts
- Manage Social Security
- Take on additional roles like POA, Trustee, and/or Social Security rep payee
- Manage caregiver schedules and their accountability
- Hire, pay, mentor, and support caregivers
- Create a system for meal prep and delivery
- Keep an inventory of all supplies for timely reordering and distribution
- Get prescriptions from a doctor for necessary medications
- Develop a system for administering medication and treating wounds
- Create a log for communication between caregivers
- Buy a nanny camera
- Set up technology for the internet, nanny cam, texting, music, and television
- Be the messenger between the patient and her friends and relatives

It's been almost five years since we started driving out to visit Sheila—half an hour each way—with a picnic basket and a cooler full of hard seltzers. We did that for two years, believing we were helping and could manage it.

Then we moved Sheila onto our property, into what you will learn about in Chapter G: The Gypsy Caravan.

Looking back, I hadn't the faintest idea what I was doing. I didn't understand what I was signing up for. This wouldn't be a part-time act of kindness; it would be an everyday job: seven days a week—cooking, preparing, and delivering meals; managing medication; navigating moods; scheduling caregivers; cleaning messes; and fielding emergencies.

I didn't expect to handle everything from food service to finance, facilities, and legal management.

My husband, Tony, managed all the construction, delivered meals, and supported me during my frequent meltdowns. We were a team; it was hard, but we had each other.

Chapter F

Fair is a 4-Letter F-Word

Saying life is fair is a ridiculous notion. Fair is a four-letter F-word. Translate it however you wish.

The F-word phrase came to life when we hired Honoré, our primary caregiver and a real-life hero in Sheila's care. I've dedicated a chapter to her. (Chapter H: Honoré).

Honoré's words weren't just something clever she said—the F-word phrase was a lesson passed down from her mother when she was a little girl. When Honoré complained that something wasn't fair, her mother responded with that same unflinching truth: "Fair is a four-letter F-word." She has carried it with her ever since.

Chapter G

Gypsy Caravan and a Gallery of Her Own

Since Sheila moved onto our property, she has lived in two of our dwellings.

The Gypsy Caravan

The first one was what we called the "Gypsy Caravan," because Sheila always thought of herself as a gypsy. It was a deluxe setup with a trailer, deck, covered roof, and a partial ocean view. At the time, we believed it would be a peaceful, private space where she could still feel independent.

The trailer we bought—and all the construction that went into the roof and deck—all done by Tony and the boys, Danny and Jason, couldn't have been completed any sooner. We got the call from Sheila's neighbor just in time. Sheila had been seen walking on the road with a brown bag of groceries in her hand, asking strangers if they'd seen a little boy.

That was it. That was the moment we knew she could no longer live alone in her house.

Tony had no issue picking her up that day and bringing her to her new home. The Gypsy Caravan awaited her—freshly built, outfitted with care, and facing the ocean. However, keeping her in it was a different story.

We were surprised to find that some aspects of the trailer were problematic. The first thing Sheila did was accidentally lock herself inside and then climb out of the bedroom window onto the deck. The first time she landed on the deck, she was somehow fine. Later that same day, though, she climbed out of the kitchen window and fell onto the stairs leading up to the deck, scraping her leg badly.

That was day one. Sheila roamed the property for the next few months, wrestling tropical flowers with her bare hands because she could no longer have a sickle or knife.

On a few occasions, she made it out to the road. She must have hitchhiked the first time because we found her two miles away at a roadside coffee and souvenir shop. She didn't remember any details, so to this day, we still don't know exactly what happened.

The second time, she flagged down a car on the highway and directed it into our driveway, where we found her flirting with two gay Englishmen and speaking with a British accent.

During the months she lived in the Gypsy Caravan, our daughters, Christie and Monyca, and a few close friends, Linda and Gena, would visit her regularly, bringing food, drinks, and their companionship. It helped keep things calm: familiar faces and small comforts.

We also had two paid caregivers: Honoré, who you'll learn more about in the next chapter, and Zoe, a very capable high school girl. Zoe was old enough to drive and was readily available to help, especially when Sheila disappeared. It was Zoe who found Sheila after hitching a ride to the coffee and souvenir shop.

For a while, our system worked. Not smoothly, not perfectly, but collectively, we got the job done.

The Gallery

In the second dwelling, we created a Gallery that showcased all of Sheila's art and collectibles. It became a place that reflected who she was, surrounding her with pieces of her life and imagination.

Tony and the boys had a lot to accomplish before we moved Sheila into the Gallery. First, we needed to sell her house—a project that came with its own emotional landmines. Decades of collectibles had to be sorted, sold, or given away.

Vintage clothing, antique furniture, and layers of memories were tucked away in every drawer. What we wanted most was to preserve her art.

But where would we put it? We had an outbuilding on the property, one that we had once lived in ourselves while building our main house. It wasn't just storage—it held history. It had potential. So that's where the art would go. That's where Sheila would go.

As it turned out, the location of the Gypsy Caravan was a mistake. We had imagined it as a peaceful spot with a nice view, close enough for us to help, far enough to give her some feeling of independence. But it backfired.

Whenever a car came down the driveway—someone visiting us, not her—Sheila would come running out, either crying or speaking in a stream of incoherent language. It wasn't just unsettling; it was scaring people off. Even those who knew her were taken aback. We realized it wasn't just inconvenient; it was unsustainable.

And then there were the breadfruit leaves. A big breadfruit tree stood between our house and the trailer, and several times a day, Sheila would go collect the dead leaves that had fallen beneath it. She carried them back to her place like they were treasures. Over time, the pile grew. Without realizing it, she created an earwig community beneath the caravan. Whoever brought the food tray back from her trailer to our house with dirty dishes for me to wash also delivered loads of earwigs. It was too much.

The Caravan was also too close to the street. All she had to do was walk down the driveway, and she'd be on the road. Once, she not only made it to the street—she crossed it. Somehow, she wandered down to a little farm stand that sold East Maui Chocolate. When we found her, she was entertaining the landowner and the man who worked there, holding court with nonsensical stories, laughing, spinning out sentences that didn't connect, and having absolutely no plan to leave.

She was perfectly at home in her confusion. We, on the other hand, were panicked. Moments like that made it clear: the Gypsy Caravan was over. It was time to move her—and fast.

All the while, we were juggling a second, full-blown operation in the background. I was selling Sheila's house—making deals with the buyers to keep feeding her cat while the escrow lingered. Christie organized the loading and unloading of years of accumulated belongings. Everything was sorted: what could be sold, what had to be tossed, and what was too meaningful to lose.

Christie piled it all up for a three-day yard sale on her property that felt more like an estate triage. She coordinated dump runs with the rest. Finally, she packed the art. Piece by piece, frame by frame, Christie, Monyca, and our friends boxed up the works that meant the most—the paintings, the dolls, the hand-stitched jewelry, and the coconuts she once sold at farm stands. It was all headed to the Gallery.

Before it could become "the Gallery," the outbuilding had to transform completely. First, Tony and the boys needed to ensure it was safe. Jason installed screens to keep out rats and bugs, knowing exactly what damage they could inflict on pictures, paintings, and delicate collectibles. One infestation could erase an entire body of work.

Then came the rest—the inside of the entire building was painted, and new vinyl floors were installed. We weren't just cleaning it up—we were giving it a second life—a space that would honor Sheila's life's work, even as her mind continued to fray.

While Sheila stayed in the trailer, her incontinence worsened. We needed a better setup—something more accessible, manageable, and dignified.

So, before she moved into the Gallery, Tony and Danny built an outdoor covered shower and toilet, tucked neatly alongside the building. They also constructed a covered front porch, which quickly became the entrance, serving not just as a way in but as a soft invitation into a new chapter.

And unlike the trailer, the ocean view was no longer partial. From the Gallery, it was the entire view. The whole horizon. It provided a sense of space and calm, even when nothing else about caregiving felt relaxed at all.

Since the Gallery took time to complete, Sheila walked there from her trailer—always accompanied by someone, of course—to admire her new building. She would step onto the porch, gaze through the entry, and take in the walls lined with her paintings, dolls, and handmade jewelry. The very best of her, preserved.

By then, she had lost all ability and desire to make art. Yet, she still possessed a keen eye for it. She would pause before specific pieces, tilt her head, and smile pensively. At times, she would express something sharp and perceptive, as if her former self still resided deep inside, just waiting for the right angle of light to shine through.

The Gallery gave her that light.

Chapter H

Honoré

The longer Honoré stayed, the more we loved her. She was a gift from heaven.

Everybody Needs an Honoré

If you're lucky, at some point in your life, you'll have an Honoré—someone who jumps into the trenches with you, fends off exhaustion with seltzers, and whose quirks become a language that you comprehend fluently and enjoy thoroughly.

Honoré made a positive impact on us. She didn't just take care of Sheila; she cared for us, too, quietly, generously, and without opposition or disagreement. Honoré purchased things for Sheila out of her own pocket and refused reimbursement. She stayed late. She listened when I revealed my fear, frustration, and sadness.

Over and over again, when I thought something wasn't fair, Honoré reminded me that fairness had nothing to do with it. Only love, endurance, and showing up every day mattered. And she was exemplary in modeling those characteristics daily.

Her work ethic was steady, unshakable, and rooted in something deeper. It was shaped by her upbringing: a strong, dedicated mother, a caring and supportive stepfather, and a family caregiving journey for her Aunt Michele that lasted fifteen long, arduous years.

I first met Honoré at a birthday party for my neighbor, Martha. She was a cool cat—quiet, had a rabbit, and gave off an air of curious caution. She said very little that evening. The mix of people at the party included her friends and mine, and I had a good time. I remember noticing her, but I wouldn't have guessed how important she would become in my life.

When Sheila moved into the Gypsy Caravan and started jumping out of windows and acting erratic, I knew I needed help. Serious help. I put the word out, and almost immediately, Honoré's name came up.

The good news? She was interested. We made a date to meet.

She later told me that she approached that first meeting with trepidation. She knew this would be a delicate and vital conversation—and she wasn't sure she'd meet my expectations.

But once I heard her story, my reaction was instant: Oh my God. She's perfect.

Honoré-isms

Once on the job, we didn't just have conversations– we had Honoré-isms — little phrases Honoré tossed around throughout the day, some clever, some sharp, and some that came from a place deeply rooted in her past. Classic Honoré is dependable and detailed, with a unique spin on words, like her unique spin on life.

"I'm going off campus..."Honoré always told me when she was leaving the property. Going off-campus was her shorthand for presence and care — but she didn't say she was leaving the property. She used "campus" as a clever twist on our ever-changing compound — a reimagined small East Maui college, where we learned, cared for others, and slept when we could.

On her way to the store, she would say, "Do you need nothing?" She had a way of asking if I needed anything, but always with the implication that sometimes, in the middle of chaos, "nothing" was probably the only thing I wanted.

"But I digress." Honoré could be in the middle of an important story, and somehow, she would pause, grin, and drop this line—a tiny reminder that sometimes changing your train of thought is half the fun.

"Fair is a four-letter F-word." There were no illusions, no sugarcoating. Honoré knew—and made sure I remembered—that fairness was a fantasy, especially in caregiving. The F-word phrase was gritty wisdom wrapped in humor.

"My Homo." When Honoré and I first met, she used the words "my homo" to describe her gay male friend back in Texas—a place where she was born and raised. She wanted me to recognize that "every badass bitch needs a homo—and he is my homo." It caught me off guard. I thought it was rude. She, in turn, thought it was peculiar when I used the word "retarded"—not to describe people with disabilities but rather to accentuate people's poor decisionmaking. She knew I had devoted my life to educational improvement and found it odd that I would use this language when a different choice of words would have sufficed.

At some point, we shrugged at each other lovingly and compromised complacently. This was just us—two imperfect people shaped by different places, times, and language styles. We decided we could live with it. Sometimes, we were rude; other times, we were just real.

"Nippie." Honoré's made-up word for a "new hippie"—usually referring (not so lovingly) to the caregiver who had reinvented herself as a self-proclaimed guru. Think tie-dye, crystals, and pretend consciousness, but little caregiving skill. "Nippie" was an inside joke, a full-body eye roll packed into two syllables. (Bless her heart, but she couldn't change a diaper if you paid her in patchouli oil.)

"Mommy." When Honoré said "Mommy," it wasn't immature. It was a glimpse of the child still living inside her, even though she was in her early forties. She missed her mom deeply—hadn't seen her in three years or returned to Texas to see her in four. Saying "Mommy" out loud was her way of reaching out across all the miles and all the longing, holding onto a piece of home she couldn't quite get back to.

Honoré-isms weren't just things she said. They were snapshots—a way to capture the hard days, the absurd moments, and the parts of life that didn't fit neatly into caregiving charts or polite conversations. Some were funny; some were witty, while others carried more weight than she ever said out loud.

But together, they reminded me that you don't get through this kind of reality by being perfect. You get through it by being real—and if you're lucky, you have someone like Honoré next to you, speaking a language that makes sense, if only to you.

Chapter I

Indifference

There comes a point in caregiving when your body shows up, but your emotions do not. It's exhausting, not because you do not care, but because you care too much. You start to detach while prepping meals for delivery, fielding complaints from every direction, and walking through yet another day of self-imprisonment.

My Indifference

I didn't call it apathy. I called it self-preservation. I responded to Sheila's bizarre behavior with a shrug and a sigh when I discovered exploded dinners in the microwave with flies, a large Tupperware bin filled with canned goods and cat urine, and a big machete she must have stolen from David. "Of course, this happened," I'd think, not due to a lack of concern but because my nervous system couldn't handle any more alarm bells.

This wasn't burnout exactly—it was something quieter and more durable. It was the slow settling of indifference, just enough to function without losing it every day. I wanted to be indifferent to cope, but I wasn't very good at it; I still cared too much to let it all go.

Sheila's Indifference

Somewhere along the line, Sheila stopped being concerned about what most people value: privacy, modesty, and social grace. She became indifferent to everything.

For example, when the caregiver arrived at the Gallery, Sheila was often found sitting on the couch, topless. She fed the cats chocolate pudding. No matter what was happening, her words always drifted back to the white birds. She pointed at them with eyes wide open, whether they existed or not. It didn't seem to matter if her language unraveled into gibberish. She spoke it anyway, as if meaning itself were beside the point.

It wasn't funny at first. But later, in the haze of my indifference, it became hysterical. Dementia has a way of bulldozing shame and decorum. And somehow, Sheila leaned into it as if she were starring in a situation comedy.

Her indifference was frustrating, but it made us laugh when we needed it most.

Sheila also became indifferent about eating with her dentures. She used to wear them every day. It made sense—she liked food, and having teeth helped her enjoy it. What an obvious notion.

However, shortly after she moved to the Gallery, many things changed. She underwent a transition from the Olympic Champion to Sedentary Sally, during which time she stopped wearing her dentures.

She simply refused. Of course, this made no sense. We were still bringing her regular meals—chicken, broccoli, and potatoes—basic, healthy food that you have to chew.

She still had a healthy appetite but acted indifferent about it. Things aren't logical in the mind of someone with dementia. Not in the way we expect them to be.

And once the dentures were out, they stayed out for days, sometimes weeks, no matter how often we reminded her or how the food was cut. She'd gum her way through it or ignore the meal entirely. It was another case of indifference where we had to stop trying to make sense of it and adapt.

Chapter J
Journals Map the Journey

I rekindled the journaling habit after retiring from the Department of Education. At the time, I was working as a grant writer for a non-profit organization called Ma Ka Hāna Ka ⬚Ike. It was during the height of the COVID-19 pandemic when for-profit and non-profit hospitals and schools around the globe were restructuring their business processes to prevent the spread of the disease.

The Executive Director, Lipoa Kahaleuahi, made a bold and compassionate call: She asked the staff to stop working for a week. She promised we would all be paid. And—she asked us to keep a journal. I have been making journal entries ever since.

Journal Entry

Why have I become less motivated to do simple tasks like filing Sheila's bank statements or clearing my desk? What will motivate me to get back in the groove?

Tony and I have become the operators of a rest home on our property. The pay is terrible, and we work seven days a week coordinating visitors, their schedules, and their pay, as well as cooking, prepping, and delivering three meals a day. It seems

51

natural that this obligation is in the way because I vowed to do three things when I retired: write, cook delicious food, and exercise for fun.

I guess these journal entries count as writing for the two-year memoir of my life dealing with Auntie's dementia—so I got that going for me, LOL.

I also saved the early conversations between Honoré and me, writing emails and texts about Sheila's progress. The communication is poetic and fun, which is great when the subject is complex.

This entry revealed what I masked—the exhaustion, frustration, resignation, and a feigned spark of resilience. I wrote it almost three years ago, and somehow, much of the sentiment still lingers. The feelings haven't left; they've just settled under the subtle weight of time.

What started as a writing assignment during the height of COVID-19 quickly transformed into a tool for survival: emotionally, mentally, and practically. Once private, these entries have begun to chart the entire journey of caregiving: the tiny rebellions, the "LOL," the dark humor that isn't funny but still helps you breathe.

Chapter K

Kaleidoscope

Life with Sheila was filled with unexpected overlaps, patterns that turned with each conversation, every shared name, every memory. It was like living inside a kaleidoscope. One turn, and suddenly, something made sense. Another turn, and it scattered again.

Sheila was an artist of many talents. She painted in every medium—watercolor, oil, acrylic created jewelry and crafted dolls. She sewed tiny handmade necklaces and earrings onto her dolls, with each piece being delicate and full of detail. She even painted coconuts, and at one point, she earned a living selling them at farm stands and local markets.

Her house in Nahiku was packed with framed photographs and artwork—giant to teeny images of people she loved, her creations, and Bart's photography. When we moved her out of her home and into the trailer, we brought over a few boxes at a time—just enough for her to admire and remember. And it worked, for a while.

But by the time she moved into the Gallery, everything had changed. She disassembled the necklaces, pried the jewels from the dolls, and concealed the jewelry in various locations—even in her food.

The kaleidoscope had shifted again. Sheila's transformation was not sudden, but it was undeniable. She went from an Olympiad—climbing stairs, chasing yard guys, stalking windows—to being practically bedridden.

She stopped coming up the hill, stopped pacing, and began lying on the couch as if it were her bed, curled up for hours or days. The kaleidoscope kept turning. Eventually, she stopped sitting up to eat. She refused to wear her dentures.

The only thing that could rouse her was that shiny chocolate wrapped in silver paper—a Hershey's kiss that Honoré would leave on the vanity as bait to entice her off the couch and into the shower. Honoré had to get her up at least once each day. As she became increasingly incontinent, she began with a daily lower-body wash and rinse.

The soulful, sadistic screaming echoed daily in the shower. It was a full-body protest—loud, relentless, primal. Sheila felt uneasy about being naked with her caregiver. Perhaps she was embarrassed. Maybe she felt afraid. Yet, it appeared as fury.

And still, Honoré and the others stayed with her, patiently guiding her through the rawest, most vulnerable part of the day. Then, as if a switch had flipped, the kaleidoscope would conclude, scattering a brilliant and colorful array of new colors. Her satanic song would subside, and Sheila would gently say, "Thank you, honey."

Chapter L

Laundry

I never got used to doing Sheila's laundry after her incontinence began. I was too sensitive to the smell, too disgusted by the waste I had to rinse from her pants. No matter how much I tried to detach or "toughen up," this part never became easier. It felt dehumanizing. For her. For me.

We made numerous updates to her wardrobe during this transition. Leggings were the first to go. You can only imagine the mess—they clung to everything: pee, poo... and any shred of dignity we were trying to preserve.

We began ordering skirts and slips to make undressing Sheila in the shower easier. Honoré joined me as my laundry partner when we moved Sheila into the Gallery. Together, we faced the war zone of soiled clothing. We made endless decisions: How do we eliminate the smell? Should we try vinegar? Should we use a deodorizer? We experimented with product after product. But bleach was the only thing that worked for me.

We strategized. We experimented. We did laundry like it was a competitive sport. Honoré also helped with the wardrobe choices, which became another thing. I had never heard of period panties before—thick, absorbent underwear that looked like boys' briefs with extra layering at the crotch. They worked during the early stages when her incontinence was mostly pee. Back when things were still manageable. Just barely.

Chapter M

Manifesting

People often roll their eyes when they hear the word manifesting. They believe it means dreaming without taking action or, worse, some form of magical thinking. However, that's not what I was doing. I was planning Sheila's new life, writing down things that needed to exist—for her and for me...

I journaled about a trailer. Drew it. Measured it. Wrote down what kind of furnishings it should have, where the ocean view would be best, and what type of shelter we'd need to build over it to feel like a real home, where peace could still take root, even as everything else was slipping away.

I sketched the layout of the structures on our property and penciled in the raised beds. I made lists of the kinds of flowers I wanted in them, not just for ornamental value but because Sheila loved color, texture, and movement. She wasn't painting anymore, but her eyes still followed beauty wherever it bloomed.

And the Gallery? That was in the journal long before we started the renovation. It wasn't a fantasy but a hope and then a plan. A vision I couldn't let go of. And then it was real. It wasn't magic. Instead, it was imagining something with so much clarity and commitment that the trailer, the Gallery, the raised beds—

everything I sketched or described—began to take shape, slowly, steadily, and sometimes serendipitously, just as I envisioned it.

Of course, I couldn't have manifested any of the buildings without the love and labor of Tony and Danny—or without Christie, who coordinated the movement of Sheila's precious artwork from her property to ours, or Jason, who installed the window screens, hung the paintings, and laid the vinyl flooring; or Gena, who initiated the cultivation of flowers and herbs in the raised beds that Tony had placed near the caravan. The practicality of manifesting something rests in the hands of people who get things done—who make the vision become a reality.

So, for me, manifesting was a process. A way to imagine and establish a new way of existence for Sheila's continued presence in her own life.

Chapter N
NannyCam

You don't just go out one day and buy a NannyCamFirst, you go through a process—a quiet storm of emotions and justifications. Even if you're not trying to spy, you are trying to watch. You're trying to know.

It starts with guilt. You wonder if it's an invasion of privacy. You ask yourself, "Would she be ashamed if she knew I was watching?" Then you move to the justifications: "I'm not trying to catch her doing something wrong. I'm trying to keep her safe." You say things like, "This is in her best interest," even though you're about to cross some invisible line.

Next comes the fear of what you might see: A fall. A meltdown. A moment that confirms your worst suspicions. You weigh the pros and cons. Where would it go? Would she notice it? Would it record sound? Could I check it from my phone? Then something happens. It's a story that doesn't match up. And suddenly, you realize: You need to know.

There are many products out there. Some NannyCams come with all the bells and whistles—motion detection, two-way audio, cloud storage, AI alerts, and night vision. You can spend hundreds on a single device. But we didn't. We chose something very inexpensive. It has a simple setup and no subscription. It connects to an app on our phones, and we can check in from anywhere. And you know what? It's been working just fine.

Zoe set it up—quick and easy. And Honoré? She's in charge of it. Of course, she is. She's the best person for surveillance. She doesn't just watch the camera. She reads the camera. She notices mood shifts, physical changes, restlessness—things most people would miss.

She's not looking for trouble. She's making sure there isn't any. But the reality is, a NannyCam can be... addicting. You think you'll only check it when you need to, but then you start checking it just in case—and then you start checking it when you shouldn't. My suggestion to Honoré—presented gently and respectfully— "When you're on a break, you can't look at the NannyCam. You have to take the break."

"I know it's hard," I told her. "I know you're highly responsible. I know you care so deeply. But you have to take care of yourself, too." Because even the best caregivers—especially the best—need a break from watching, even if someone still requires supervision.

The NannyCam wasn't just for peace of mind—it saved time, energy, and hot meals. For instance, when Sheila pretended to sleep in the mornings, Honoré would use the camera to check before bringing over a warm breakfast. No longer would she watch her meals go cold or feel frustrated when Sheila feigned sleep because she wasn't interested in having company.

The NannyCam shifted from being about "watching" to managing the chaos—quietly, smartly, and with just enough distance to prevent things from unraveling. Anyone in my situation should get a NannyCam. You can determine how to use it and who is responsible for it, but it's essential to understand what's happening in this person's unpredictable life. Dementia doesn't provide updates. The NannyCam does.

Chapter O

Open the Drapes

Remember the Olympic Champion? That phase of my year-long time with Sheila forced me to confront the intense fear I felt when she stalked us. I wasn't just closing the curtains—I was barricading our peace. I used adhesive Velcro tape to draw the drapes and seal them shut when I saw her coming.

I hid from her, tucked into corners of the house where no window or door offered a view. Out of sight, out of reach, and barely holding it together. By then, I had switched to Maui Hard Seltzers. Dragon fruit was my favorite. I'd crack one open and sip it slowly, waiting for the storm to pass. Sometimes, she'd leave in a few minutes. Other times, she'd linger for an hour, pacing, moaning, and staring through the glass.

Velcroed drapes. Locked doors. A hard seltzer in hand. This was my normal. Fortunately for me, Sheila's status as an Olympic champion was waning. At first, she only came up the hill sometimes. Then, she came up less frequently. Eventually, she stopped coming altogether. By the end of those months, she had stopped coming altogether. It was then that I opened the drapes.

I continually surprised myself. Oh my gosh, the drapes are open! This is so great—such a relief. I could feel the tropical breeze again. But it wasn't that great for her. Sheila had taken many falls that year. Somehow, those falls flipped a switch in her brain—one that made her realize, dimly and flickering, that she couldn't jet off anymore. I'm not sure that's even possible with a dementia patient. But it seems like what happened.

Chapter P

Pee, Poo, Panties, and Polident

Honoré and I shared many things in common—two in particular: I perseverated, and she overthought. Those two forces—mine and hers—guided us in all our final decisions: the right shower chair, the right wardrobe, and the right menu for nourishment. We went through a series of discussions about the shower chair. The first chair we received was basic: a white plastic seat, silver adjustable legs, and a blue foam back and seat. We thought it was ideal—comfortable, stable, and easy to clean.

But it wasn't long before Sheila began tearing off the foam. She'd sit there, mid-shower, and pick at it compulsively, stripping it down as if she had a nervous tic. Of course, that led to more conversations. "Should we get one without foam?" "Was the foam irritating her skin?" "Was it sensory?" "Should we glue it back?" "Can you even glue foam?"

After a few unsuccessful attempts to find the perfect shower chair, we settled on one that wasn't elegant but was absolutely necessary: a padded toilet seat commode. Why? Because Sheila was defecating on all the other chairs. The standard chairs lacked a toilet hole, and cleaning them turned into a daily nightmare. We removed the bucket from the new commode so the waste could fall straight to the ground. Mercifully, it was an outdoor shower, where a hose and a few deep breaths could make everything clean again.

And there was a hidden bonus: when the water was aimed just right through the open seat, it hit its target perfectly—Sheila's bum, rinsed and ready, with minimal fuss. The new chair wasn't just about hygiene—it was about completing the job in a way that preserved Sheila's dignity, alleviating caregivers from the burden of supporting her weight while spraying her down, and now effectively and efficiently addressing the target area.

In contrast, transitioning to Sheila wearing diapers—or "panties," as we referred to them—wasn't one of our decisions; it was Lila's. Lila was the granddaughter of Gena, a young college student studying nursing. Her mind worked like a textbook. She absorbed everything methodically, clinically, and accurately. As a caregiver, she didn't get caught in emotional spirals or lengthy debates. She simply did what needed to be done.

When Honoré and I hesitated—still discussing timing, dignity, brands, and sizes—Lila showed up with a pack of adult diapers she'd bought herself. "This is what Sheila needs," she said. No drama. No overthinking. Just the right move, right on time. That's how wearing "panties" began. And Sheila has been wearing them ever since.

Similarly, Honoré didn't overthink the need for a cleaning solution for Sheila's dentures, and I didn't dwell on it. She said we needed something to clean Sheila's dentures, and I immediately went on Amazon to search. I chose the brand you've heard of for decades—Polident. Specifically, the kind that fizzes like Alka-Seltzer and promises results in three seconds. It seemed simple enough. At that point, simplicity was the goal.

But before Sheila insisted that she would no longer wear her dentures, there was a stage when she adamantly refused to take them out. They remained in for days. Honoré was concerned—not just for hygiene but for dignity.

We already had the Polident; we just needed the teeth in the glass. The next day, Sheila was in full rebellion. She refused to undress, refused to be bathed, and defiantly refused to part with her dentures. She expressed her resistance like a wild animal, twisting, shouting, and clenching her jaw.

Then, in a miraculous moment of chaos disguised as divine intervention, she lunged forward, mouth open wide, aiming to bite Honoré. However, instead of making contact, her dentures flew from her mouth and hit the floor. Honoré, ever the professional, didn't flinch. She smiled, scooped them up and dropped them into a glass of water, where they fizzed like a tiny geyser of victory.

Chapter Q
Quality of Life

This memoir fundamentally focuses on preserving Sheila's quality of life. Not the kind measured in data or framed by neat little checklists—but the messy, beautiful, moment-to-moment kind. The kind you fight for in small gestures: warm meals, open drapes, clean clothes, and fresh flowers in a jar. The type of life you create when dignity seems to be slipping, yet you hold it up with routines, laughter, patience, and sheer will.

My husband and I, along with our daughters, friends, and caregivers—took that responsibility seriously. We weren't trying to extend Sheila's life; instead, we aimed to fill it with light, color, comfort, sufficient structure to keep her safe, and enough softness to let her feel human. For us, quality of life became less about milestones and more about moments. A good shower, a quiet afternoon, a look of recognition, a well-timed joke—that was success. That was care.

Chapter R

Rage!

One of the most well-known stories in the study of brain trauma and behavioral change is that of Phineas Gage. He was a mild-mannered and responsible railroad construction foreman. In 1848, a terrible accident changed everything. While packing explosive powder into rock with a tamping iron, the charge ignited and sent the iron rod, which was over three feet long, through his skull.

It entered through his cheek and exited through the top of his head. Miraculously, he survived. However, the man who recovered was not the person his friends and coworkers remembered. Once respectful and even-tempered, Gage became impulsive, irritable, and prone to fits of rage. His drastic personality shift became one of the earliest documented cases linking brain trauma, specifically to the frontal lobe, to significant behavioral and emotional changes.

I often thought of Phineas Gage when trying to understand Sheila's most volatile moments. She, too, had suffered trauma to the brain—not from an iron rod, but through the slow, silent damage of dementia and Alzheimer's. And like Gage, she sometimes became unrecognizable. The disease rewired her reactions. Her fury wasn't always her—it was the disorder speaking through her, just as it did with him.

Chapter S

Sacrifice, Sarcasm, and Satire

My mom used the word "sacrifice" daily. To her, it was one of the most important behavioral qualities a good person could possess. We were all expected to learn how to sacrifice, just as Jesus had sacrificed his life so that we could go to heaven.

Every year, the month leading up to Easter signified Lent. That's when she ensured we sacrificed something. Usually, it was candy. As we got a little older, she allowed us more freedom. We could choose our own sacrifice, but we still had to feel its impact. It had to cost something.

Sacrifice became a way of life. We always gave something up—time, comfort, pleasure, ease. It was ingrained in our upbringing, a silent rule we all lived by. In high school, I volunteered at a center for women with mental disabilities. At that time, I attended a Catholic girls' school, and a nun would drive me and a few classmates to the facility to teach the women about Catholicism. It was framed as a service.

Sacrifice became normalized for me—just part of the routine of life. But alongside it, something else was taking shape: a new sense of humor I acquired through observation. And that's where the sarcasm crept in. I hadn't thought it through until recently, but I found myself crediting my mother. Is that where we all got it? The sarcasm manifested differently among her seven children, like seven variations on a theme. Mine was slightly subtle and disguised, but it was still there. It snuck into my tone, timing, and take on the world. It made me laugh, and it kept me sane.

With Sheila, I sacrificed more than just time and energy. I sacrificed sleep, boundaries, and even parts of my identity— sometimes willingly, but most times not. And when it all became too overwhelming, sarcasm stood by like an old friend in the room, rolling its eyes right alongside me. Similarly, coordinating the mind-boggling number of responsibilities involved in running a rest home had become a kind of satire—this story that intertwined sacrifice, sarcasm, and the uncertain reality of caring for someone with dementia.

In caring for Sheila, my perspective on satire revealed the quiet absurdities caregivers faced while navigating a system steeped in routines, repetition, and relentless loss. It became a fragile form of relief—a way to laugh through tears, to name the madness without succumbing to it. In those moments, the line between tragedy and comedy blurred, and the caregiving experience adopted a strangely satirical edge. Finding humor in the distress was the only way to keep going—the only way to feel okay again.

Chapter T

Mr.T

Mr. T is my husband, T for Tony. Honoré gave him that name. Initially, she called him Mr. Wonderful, but I vetoed it. It sounded too sarcastic—So, we landed on Mr. T. But not that Mr. T! —Our Mr. T didn't wear gold bling, but he was strong, steady, and showed up when it mattered most. He built things, fixed things, cooked meals, and lifted burdens. He was my partner in every sense of the word—through five years of courting, over forty years of marriage, and now, through the thick of caregiving.

In his youth, Tony liked his family, but wasn't especially attached to them. His father was a traveling salesman, often gone, and his mother, from England, had her own way of doing things. When Tony and his friends got stoned in high school, she'd make them grilled cheese sandwiches on sourdough without judgment. On school mornings, she'd fold his clothes and lay them out neatly for him to wear that day. It was thoughtful but distant, polite love wrapped in dependence and tea towels.

It was nothing like my house. In my home, we had Catholic parents and Catholic rules. On Good Friday, we knelt in front of the Blessed Mother statue with the drapes closed, honoring Jesus' death on the cross in silence and reverence. We said the rosary together. There was no getting high, no munchies, no soft landings, just sacrifice, ritual, and an ever-present sense of guilt if you got it wrong.

When Tony and I were in our first year together in high school, I told my mother, "I adore Tony!" She snapped back at me with a threatening face, "You adore no one but God!" I never got tired of Tony. He was very funny, really smart, and authentically in love with me, which was perfect. And now, decades later, we do this thing with Sheila together. It isn't easy. But it's okay—for me—because of him.

Chapter U

Unpredictable and Unreliable

Sheila wasn't the only unpredictable one in this story. A few of the caregivers we hired—especially the ones who didn't last long—could give Sheila a run for her money. They came with glowing resumes, dramatic stories, and big promises. We heard about decades of experience, advanced degrees, world travel, intuitive healing, and deep empathy. Sometimes, it felt like we were interviewing an unaccomplished actress disguised as a medical professional.

But the reality? Most of their stories were exaggerated. One highly educated woman could rarely find a ride. Her car broke down repeatedly. She threw up once a month. But there were never any advanced warnings—only morning-of text messages that left us scrambling.

She was really good with Sheila, and Sheila really liked her when she came. But that was the problem: she didn't come consistently. There was no reliability, no accountability—just unpredictability. And that was the saddest part: we couldn't keep her, even though she did the job well when she showed up.

Once, she pulled into our driveway with a baby goat trotting behind her! A few minutes later, she appeared at my office door to inform me that a goat had followed her into the driveway and was now trapped inside her car. Then, believing the situation was under control, she went on her merry way down to see Sheila.

The windows were rolled down to give the goat fresh air, but they were rolled down too far, and the goat jumped out. Our two dogs, bigger than their intruder, exploded into motion, barking ferociously as the baby goat tore across the property, screeching and wailing in terror. Using insanity as a motivational technique, Tony corralled the dogs, rescued the goat, and put it back in the car, restoring what was left of the morning.

Sweating, with blue eyes glaring, he didn't waste words. "Stay with the goat," he said, before charging down to Sheila's to find the caregiver—and the keys. I had a moment of calm with the goat, petting its super soft and clean fur until it jumped from the back seat into the front seat and then halfway out the passenger window. Miraculously, Tony appeared. He pushed the goat back inside, tossed me the keys, and I managed to roll up the windows high enough to stop another jailbreak.

Tony turned around, wiped the sweat from his forehead, and said, "I'm sorry, Sooz. I'm such a freak." "No worries, Tone," I told him. "You did everything. "Later, we laughed—not just at the goat or the chaos it created but also at the unpredictable nature of well-meaning caregivers.

We also employed a woman who couldn't do the shower part of the morning duty. She never said she couldn't, but we found out when Honoré walked over to check on her. That wasn't something Honoré did regularly, but her intuition must've been buzzing that day.

This caregiver was reputable and kind to Sheila, but we needed her to handle the challenging task of addressing hygiene issues. We had already informed her—we called her "Nippie" (short for new hippie)—that there was a NannyCam on the lanai where Sheila spent most of her time. So, she moved to the Gallery to use her phone, a place where she couldn't be seen.

Unpredictable and unreliable. And when you're already dealing with a person with dementia—whose moods and demands shift by the minute—the last thing you need is a caregiver who can't be counted on, no matter how good her intentions are.

Chapter V

Victories, Big and Small

Amid caregiving chaos and unpredictability, we found joy in the victories. Not every victory was loud. Most were quiet, barely noticeable at the moment but a fond memory in hindsight. Sometimes, a victory looked like Sheila welcoming a visitor by sitting up and smiling or making it to the shower without resistance. Sometimes, it was a whole night's sleep without incident or remembering something that really happened.

The bigger victories took shape over time. Keeping Sheila safe, keeping her cared for, and keeping ourselves intact through all of it—those were hard-earned wins. And they weren't just ours. They belonged to the team that showed up, stepped in, and stayed. Every time someone didn't give up on her, us, or themselves, it counted. It still does. We didn't win at everything. But we learned to recognize when we did—and to let even the most minor victories mean something.

Chapter W

What Worked and What Didn't

Reflecting on our caregiving journey, we discovered clear lessons—some things held us up, others pulled us down. This chapter revisits themes from Chapters A to V and sorts them into two honest lists: what worked and what didn't.

What Worked

- Coping Mechanisms: Creating small rituals—like sharing a funny story, enjoying a great meal, or drinking a hard seltzer—provided momentary relief when things felt like they were falling apart.
- Caring Daughters and Friends: Having supportive people around us who consistently showed up, stayed late, offered their help, and asked for nothing in return was crucial to our success.
- Dignity: Maintaining the dignity of a person suffering from dementia contributed to her quality of life.
- Expectations: Knowing what to anticipate facilitated the ability to be present and adapt with greater ease.
- Honoré: Finding the right primary caregiver gave us peace of mind—and someone to lean on.

- Journaling: Engaging in written exploration of our emotions, decisions, and challenges made them significantly more manageable.

- Manifesting: Transforming outbuildings and reimagining architecture allowed us to create sustainable living spaces with purpose and intention.

- Nannycam: Installing a budget-friendly surveillance tool minimized wasted effort and uncovered gaps in coverage.

- Panties and Polident: Maintaining hygienic practices instilled comfort and organization in our daily routines.

- Sacrifice, Sarcasm, and Satire: Identifying the absurdities, laughing when we wanted to scream, and navigating through dark humor helped preserve our mental well-being.

- Mr. T: Relying on Tony—my partner through it all—kept me grounded, facilitated progress, and loved me through the toughest times of our lives, ultimately bringing us even closer together.

What Didn't Work

- Dignity: Recognizing a lack of compassion in myself and others became a valuable lesson in personal growth. Kindness mattered more when Sheila was in her most vulnerable state, regardless of whether that kindness was reciprocated.

- Expectations: Grappling with uncertainty and facing challenges we hadn't imagined was paralyzing. We expected

81

it to get harder, but not in so many unexpected and personal ways.

- Indifference: Attempting not to care was its own form of survival, but it didn't work. My emotional distance cracked under the weight of reality, and Sheila's indifference reminded me how powerless I was to change her perception or behavior.

- Unpredictable and Unreliable: Counting on unreliable individuals exhausted our energy, making it difficult to restore.

Chapter X

Xylophone

Life with dementia is like playing a xylophone. You strike a key and hope it produces a sound you recognize. Sometimes it does—clear, familiar, almost sweet. But other times, the sound is jarring or flat, leaving you unsure which note you hit. You try again, wishing the rhythm will make sense this time.

The keys are wooden and worn smoothly through repetition. Just like your hands. Just like your patience. Caregiving becomes a form of improvisation—one note at a time, striving to create harmony from something that feels endlessly offbeat. The routine never remains routine. The reactions never stay the same. And yet, you keep showing up, tapping out another day, another meal, another cleanup, another conversation—wondering if it will strike a chord or echo into silence.

Chapter Y

Yes!

Yes, to Sheila.

Yes, when she said something imaginary.

Yes, when the words were nonsense.

Yes, to her needs and changing ways.

Yes, we accept you. Yes, you are loved.

We said yes even when Sheila asked for a banana with peanut butter dipped in vinegar, followed by questions about the white birds that weren't there When she asked, "Are the sandwiches wearing necklaces of indigo and straw?"—yes. Yes, it was a way to soothe the storm. It was a bridge. A balm. A survival strategy. It didn't mean agreement. It meant peace.

Yes, to Honoré.

Yes, whatever she wanted for Sheila, whatever she needed for herself.

Yes, to her judgment. Yes, to her instincts.

Yes, to her staying sane while holding down the fort.

She was the kind of person who'd say,"I'm fine, " while carrying three grocery bags, prepping medications, cleaning a wound, and checking on the camera footage with determination and perseverance. Saying yes to her wasn't just about trust. It was a necessity. When Honoré suggested something, she wasn't guessing. She knew. So, when she asked for time, space, or even just a seltzer with me, my answer was always yes. Her requests were never burdens; they were small doorways into grace. And I was happiest when I could open them.

Yes, to my daughters and friends who volunteered.

Yes, so they knew they didn't have to do this.

Yes, they could have a break. Yes, whatever they need.

Yes, anything.

They weren't just helpers—they were lifelines. They showed up with children in arms, seltzers in coolers, conversation starters, and casseroles to die for. When they asked, "Can I trade shifts?"—yes. Yes, to swapping, yes, to venting without apology. Yes, to walking out the door without guilt. Yes, to whatever they needed to survive the moment, stay human, and remain whole.

Yvonne

Some people in my life said yes to helping Sheila from afar. Yvonne, from California, was one of them. Before Sheila had dementia, she kept in close contact with Yvonne, a dear friend of Mum's and a fellow member of the Daughters of the British Empire.

After Mum died, Sheila and Yvonne shared stories over the phone and through letters for years until Sheila stopped responding. When that happened, Yvonne emailed me to ask if everything was all right.

After learning about Sheila's prognosis, she said, "Oh dear, is there anything I can do?" I asked if she would be willing to write Sheila a brief email with pictures attached — maybe once a month or so.

It wasn't much, but it meant the world to Sheila.

This small connection stirred her long-term memory. Sheila would read Yvonne's messages repeatedly and study the pictures I printed from the emails, letting them pull her back into a world she still recognized. Yvonne knew exactly how to spark Sheila's memory and make her feel included, even from across an ocean of time and change.

Chapter Z

Zillions More to Do

We're at another crossroadsSheila's not bedridden—not yet. She's still able to make her way to the shower with help, where she delivers her daily performance of soulful satanic screaming. And honestly? The fact that she still belts it out means she hasn't fully surrendered. Not yet. There's still a fight in her. There's still noise. There's still something to wrangle.

So, what's ahead? I don't know. I never do. But I've surrendered to that—to the not knowing. I've surrendered to the idea that this is my role. And more than that, I've embraced it. I've accepted it so entirely, so repeatedly, so fiercely... It's almost like I like it.

Almost. Because underneath the rituals, meltdowns, decision trees, and dirty laundry, there's always one thing left to do. And when that's done? Another. And another. There are zillions more to do.

Conclusion

This caregiving journey has taken you through an alphabet of experiences—from A to Z. Every letter held a story, a lesson, and a letting go. Though this book ends here, caregiving continues in all its darkness, beauty, sadness, and grace. Carry whatever you need from these pages and leave the rest behind.

Inhale the blue and let out the grey. Breathe. Whether you have support or are on your own, I hope this book reminds you that your giving matters. You are not alone. I see you. Your strength is not invisible. Your exhaustion is valid. Surrender to vulnerability and let it soften, not break you. You are doing the work of many with the hands and heart of one. There are countless things to do, but you've done enough for now.

Eat, laugh, take breaks, and breathe—and don't forget to drink water between seltzers!

www.ingramcontent.com/pod-product-compliance
Lightning Source LLC
Chambersburg PA
CBHW071212120626
46546CB00006B/2519